My first email guide

Chris Oxlade

Heinemann
LIBRARY

www.heinemann.co.uk/library

Visit our website to find out more information about Heinemann Library books.

To order:

☎ Phone 44 (0) 1865 888066

🖹 Send a fax to 44 (0) 1865 314091

💻 Visit the Heinemann Bookshop at www.heinemann.co.uk/library to browse our catalogue and order online.

First published in Great Britain by Heinemann Library, Halley Court, Jordan Hill, Oxford OX2 8EJ, part of Harcourt Education.
Heinemann is a registered trademark of Harcourt Education Ltd.

Editorial: Isabel Thomas, Charlotte Guillain and Diyan Leake
Design: Philippa Jenkins
Illustrations: Tower Designs (UK) Ltd
Picture Research: Melissa Allison
Production: Duncan Gilbert

Originated by Dot Gradations
Printed and bound in China by South China Printing Co. Ltd

13 digit ISBN 978 0 431 90698 0

11 10 09 08 07
10 9 8 7 6 5 4 3 2 1

British Library Cataloguing in Publication Data
Oxlade, Chris
My first email guide. - (My First Computer Guides)
1. Electronic mail systems - Juvenile literature
I. Title
004.6'92

A full catalogue record for this book is available from the British Library.

Acknowledgements
The publishers would like to thank the following for permission to reproduce photographs: Alamy pp. **5** right (BananaStock), **27** (Helene Rogers); Corbis pp. **24** (RF), **20** (Renee Lynn); Getty Images pp. **5** (Asia Images), **22** (Iconica), **9** bottom; Harcourt Education Ltd pp. **7** inset, **9** top, **17**, **18**, **25** (Tudor Photography); Masterfile pp. **14** (Chad Johnston), **29** (Kevin Dodge), **23**; Superstock p. **28** (age fotostock)

Cover photograph of arrows on computer keys, reproduced with permission of Corbis Royalty-Free.

The publishers would like to thank Robert Eiffert for his assistance in the preparation of this book.

Every effort has been made to contact copyright holders of any material reproduced in this book. Any omissions will be rectified in subsequent printings if notice is given to the publishers.

Contents

Some words are shown in bold, **like this**. You can find out what they mean by looking in the glossary.

What is email?

An email is a message, like a letter. You write it on a computer. You send it to another person's computer for that person to read. "Email" is short for electronic mail.

Send	Save

To: Anwar.Kalra@ntlworld.com

Add Cc | Add Bcc

Subject: Football

Attach a file   Add event info

B *I* U F T T T ⧉ ∞ ≣ ≣ ⊏ ⊐ " ≣ ≣ ≣ I× « Plain text   Check spelling ▾

Hey Anwar

Let's watch the match this afternoon.

Joe

Send	Save

This is an email message.

Email is an important way of sending messages today. Around the world, millions of emails are sent every minute.

Using email

People use email to keep in touch with friends and family members. They also use it at work and school, to send information and to organize meetings.

To: said.ali@alifamily.com
Add Cc | Add Bcc
Subject: Thanks

Dear Grandpa,
Thank you very much for the books you sent me. They are lovely. I will enjoy reading them.
Love Aliyah

To: mattjones@jonesfamily.co.uk
Add Cc | Add Bcc
Subject: Great game

Hi Matt
Great game yesterday,
See you next week
Zaki

To: anna.david@hurstschool.com
Add Cc | Add Bcc
Subject: staff meeting

Staff meeting agenda

1. School dinners
2. Assembly
3. End of term party

Email can be better for sending messages than the post. An email message arrives in a few seconds, even when it is sent to the other side of the world. Email is also cheaper to send.

| Send | Save |

To: anna.david@davidhome.com

Add Cc | Add Bcc

Subject: Bonnie

Attach a file

B I U F▾ ₸T▾ 🗏🗏 🔗 ☰☰ ⫷ ⫸ " ☰☰☰ Tₓ « Plain text

Hello Auntie,
Here is a photo I took of my new pet rabbit, called Bonnie.
Love from Claire

| Send | Save |

You can easily send photographs with your emails.

The right address

An email must be addressed to the right person, just like a letter. The address is called an **email address**.

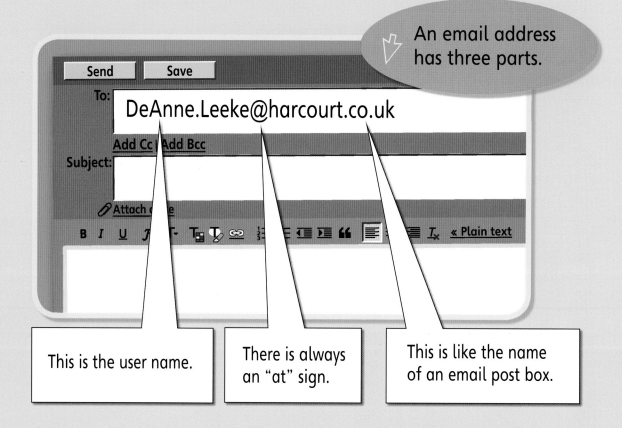

An email address has three parts.

DeAnne.Leeke@harcourt.co.uk

This is the user name.

There is always an "at" sign.

This is like the name of an email post box.

People have to set up an email address to send and receive email. Email addresses are much shorter than postal addresses!

Joe Smith
10 Hill Street
Greenville, TX
80600

Post is sometimes called "snail mail" because it is so slow compared to email!

Email programs

You need an email **program** on your computer to send and receive emails. A program is something that tells a computer what to do.

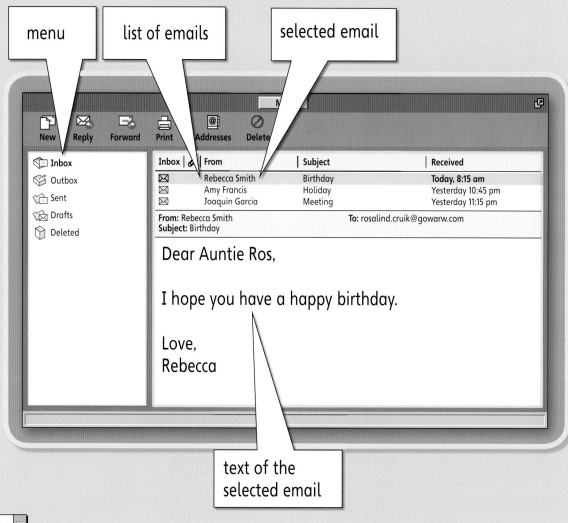

menu

list of emails

selected email

| | | New | Reply | Forward | Print | Addresses | Delete |

Inbox
Outbox
Sent
Drafts
Deleted

Inbox	From	Subject	Received
	Rebecca Smith	Birthday	**Today, 8:15 am**
	Amy Francis	Holiday	Yesterday 10:45 pm
	Joaquin Garcia	Meeting	Yesterday 11:15 pm

From: Rebecca Smith   **To:** rosalind.cruik@gowarw.com
Subject: Birthday

Dear Auntie Ros,

I hope you have a happy birthday.

Love,
Rebecca

text of the
selected email

An email program stores your emails. You can check to see all the messages you have sent or that people have sent to you.

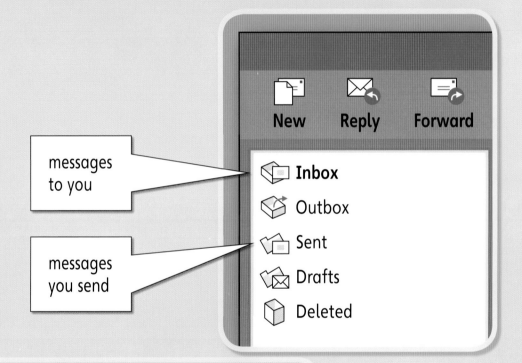

New   Reply   Forward

messages to you → Inbox
Outbox
messages you send → Sent
Drafts
Deleted

Activity
Go to a computer and click on the buttons for the Inbox, Outbox and Sent box. What emails are in them?

Writing a message

When you write a new email, first click on the "New" button. Then type in the **email address** of the person you are sending the message to. You might find that person's address in the address book on the screen.

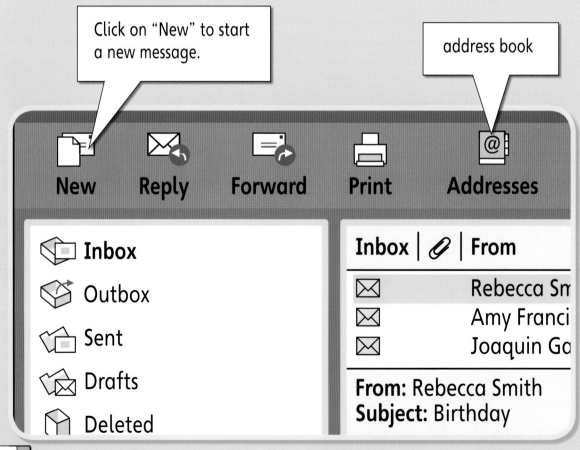

Click on "New" to start a new message.

address book

New   Reply   Forward   Print   Addresses

Inbox
Outbox
Sent
Drafts
Deleted

Inbox | 🖉 | From

Rebecca Sm
Amy Franci
Joaquin Ga

From: Rebecca Smith
Subject: Birthday

Click in the "Subject" space and write what your message is about. Next, click in the message space. Now you can start writing your message.

Send	Save		
To:	sarah.patrick@patcorp.com		

Add Cc | Add Bcc

Subject: package sent

🖉 Attach a file   🔲 Add event info

B *I* <u>U</u>   F- TT-   Tₐ 🖋 ⚯   ⊟ ⊟ ⬜ ⬛   66   ▤ ▥ ▦   Iₓ   « Plain text   Check spelling ▾

Dear Sarah

I have sent the package and you should receive it tomorrow.

Best wishes,
Sam

Send	Save

STAY SAFE   X

⚠ Never put your telephone number or other details in an email to a person you do not know.

Being polite

Remember, somebody will read the emails you write. Your emails should always be polite and easy to understand. Use complete sentences and the right punctuation.

Send   Save

To: peter.thomas@thomasfamilycom

Add Cc | Add Bcc

Subject: no news

Attach a file

B *I* U ℱ·ₜT· Tₐ ✏ ⚭ ☰ ☰ ⬅ ➡ 66 ☰ ☰ ☰ Iₓ « Plain text

IT WAS REALLY QUIET IN SCHOOL TODAY.

Never write emails in capital letters. It is like shouting in an email.

You can use special email pictures to say if you are happy, sad, angry, or surprised. These pictures are called **emoticons**. People who use email will understand what emoticons mean.

Email styles

When you write an email, think about who you are writing it to. Imagine you are talking to this person as you write.

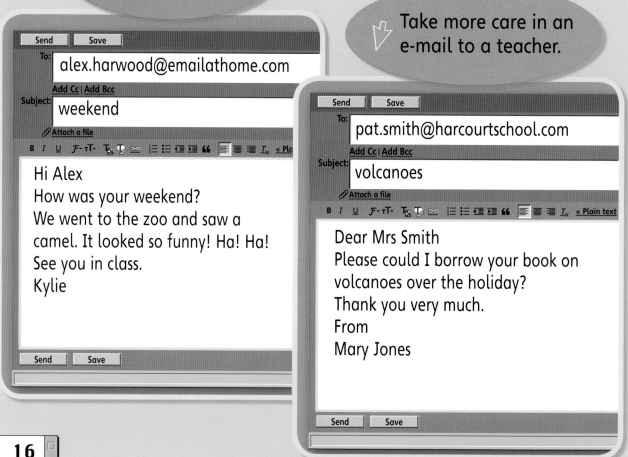

Simple notes are okay for friends.

To: alex.harwood@emailathome.com

Subject: weekend

Hi Alex
How was your weekend?
We went to the zoo and saw a camel. It looked so funny! Ha! Ha!
See you in class.
Kylie

Take more care in an e-mail to a teacher.

To: pat.smith@harcourtschool.com

Subject: volcanoes

Dear Mrs Smith
Please could I borrow your book on volcanoes over the holiday?
Thank you very much.
From
Mary Jones

Sometimes it might be better not to use email. Sometimes it is better to write a letter or card and send it in the post. Sometimes it is better to talk on the phone.

Activity
How would you write an email to your grandmother to say thank you for a present?

Send!

When you have finished writing your email, you have to send it. Read your message first to make sure you have not made any mistakes. Check to make sure that the address is right.

| Send | Save |

To:

Click on the "Send" button to send your email.

After you press the "Send" button, the computer will tell you that your message has been sent. You might hear a noise when it has gone. The computer then moves the message into the Sent box.

New Reply Forward Print Addresses

📁 Inbox

📂 Outbox

📁 Sent

📁 Drafts

📦 Deleted

Inbox | 📎 | From

✉ Rebecca S
✉ Amy Fran
✉ Joaquin G

From: Rebecca Smith
Subject: Birthday

Click here to see messages you have sent before.

Getting your mail

To find out if anybody has sent you an email, you ask the computer to look for you. Any new email messages you get go into your Inbox.

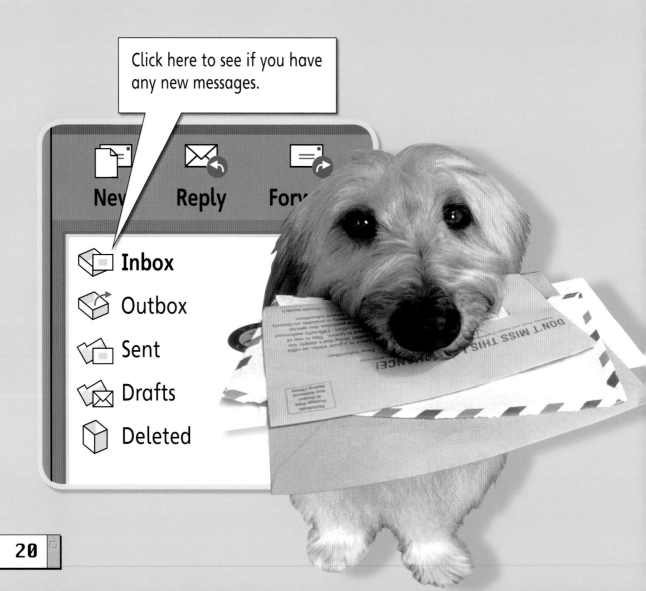

Click here to see if you have any new messages.

New   Reply   Forward

Inbox
Outbox
Sent
Drafts
Deleted

You read a message by clicking on it in the Inbox. The message usually appears on the screen underneath.

Mail		
🖨 Print	@ Addresses	⊘ Delete

Inbox	📎	From	Subject
✉		**Sarah**	**Football club**
✉		**Dan**	**Computer book**
✉		Rebecca	Birthday party

From: Rebecca Smith
Subject: Birthday

Messages you have not looked at are marked in bold.

Junk mail

When you have an **email address**, you often get emails from people you do not know. These are called **junk mail**, or **spam**. Most junk mail is trying to sell things.

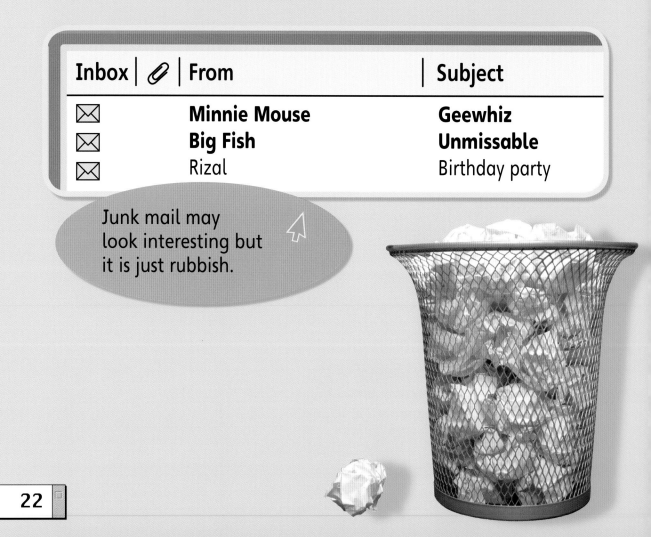

Inbox	📎	From	Subject
✉		**Minnie Mouse**	**Geewhiz**
✉		**Big Fish**	**Unmissable**
✉		Rizal	Birthday party

Junk mail may look interesting but it is just rubbish.

Be very careful with junk mail. Click on the "Delete" button straight away without reading it. It sometimes can harm your computer.

Ask an adult to help you get rid of junk mail.

Adding attachments

You can send other files with your message, such as photographs, paintings or word processor files. The files are called **attachments**.

Click on the paper clip to add an attachment.

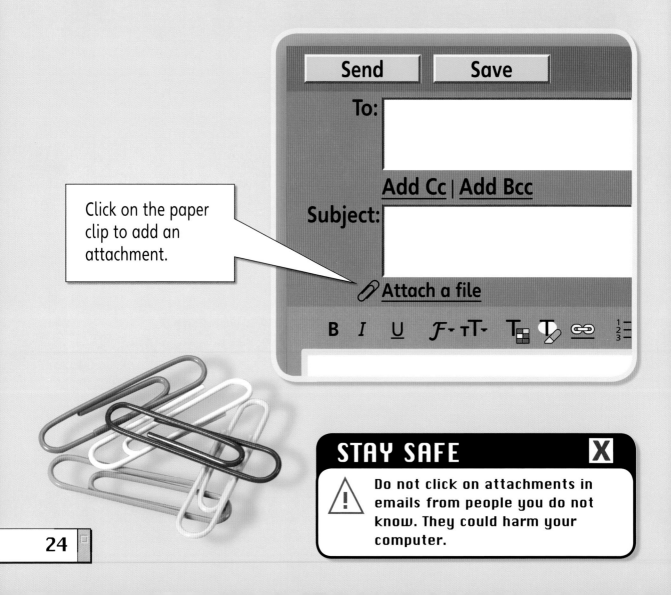

Send	Save

To:

Add Cc | Add Bcc

Subject:

⌘ Attach a file

B *I* U ℱ▾ ᴛT▾ T T ⊙ ¹₂³

STAY SAFE ☒

⚠ Do not click on attachments in emails from people you do not know. They could harm your computer.

This email has one attachment.

Activity

Ask someone to photograph you with a **digital camera**. Can you attach the photograph to an email and send it to a relative?

Other types of message

Email is not the only way of getting in touch by computer. Another way is called instant messaging. This is like talking to friends, but instead of saying things, you write them down.

What you type shows in the window. So do your friend's replies.

Instant Message

Sarah: Are you going to the party this afternoon?

Rosie: Yes, do you want a lift?

Sarah: Yes, please, what time will you be here to pick me up?

Rosie: About 6.30. What are you taking as a present?

Sarah: A box of chocolates, she is crazy about chocolate, what are you taking?

Rosie: A tee-shirt in her favourite colour.

Text messaging is similar to email. Text messaging is when you send text messages from one mobile phone to another. You use phone numbers instead of **email addresses**.

Staying safe

Email is a great way to keep in touch with your family and friends. But it is important to stay safe when you use email.

Remember:
- always delete **junk mail**
- never give your **email address** to strangers, for example on a **website**
- never agree to meet up with a stranger who emails you.

Nothing beats chatting to your friends in person.

Fun facts
about email

- The first email was sent in 1971. It was very different to the email we use today.
- Around 171 billion emails are sent every day.
- About 1.1 billion people around the world use email.

More books to read

Learn ICT: Communicate Online, Anne Rooney (QED, 2004)

Shooting Stars: Communication Crazy, Anne Rooney (Chrysalis, 2003)

Glossary

attachment file that you send with an email message

digital camera camera that takes photographs which can be put onto a computer

email address address that a person needs to send and receive emails

emoticons pictures you can add to emails to show how you feel

junk mail email messages sent from people you do not know

program set of instructions that tells a computer what to do

spam junk mail from people you do not know

website collection of linked pages on the Internet about a subject or organization

Index